The Salmon Stream

Written by Keith Pigdon
Series Consultant: Linda Hoyt

WorldWise®
Content-based Learning

T0360025

Contents

Introduction

It is early summer in Katmai National Park in Alaska. Thousands and thousands of Pacific salmon travel out of the great Pacific Ocean, where they have spent most of their lives. They swim in rivers and gather in lakes, before entering the cold mountain streams.

These salmon come together with brown bears in a dramatic way at a particular time each year. This book tells us about each of these animals and explains how and why they need each other in this freshwater salmon stream environment.

Chapter 1

Pacific salmon: An amazing life

Beginning the journey

Every year in early summer, Pacific salmon travel from the Pacific Ocean to the mountain streams of Alaska. The streams seem to fill with fish. There are so many large salmon here that there could not possibly be enough food for them in the stream. But the salmon do not need to eat, for each fish has enough food stored inside its body to complete the greatest journey of its life.

Amazingly, adult salmon, which have spent years travelling in the Pacific Ocean, can find their way back to the very stream in which they were born. Each stream has its own special smell that guides these mighty salmon back to their birthplace.

The adult salmon return to the stream where they were born to **reproduce**. These quiet waters make ideal **spawning grounds** for the salmon, as there are fewer **predators** than in the ocean to take the eggs or young fish.

A difficult time

The journey from the ocean to the salmon stream is incredibly difficult. The strong salmon have to travel through fast **rapids**, swimming against the flow of the stream. The fish always seem to swim against the **current** where the water runs swiftly from high up in the mountains down towards the ocean.

Salmon gather in the lake before beginning their journey upstream.

Alaska

Katmai National Park

Pacific Ocean

Canada

USA

Did you know?

In the ocean, Pacific salmon are all silver-coloured. However, in the mountain streams, their colours may change to red, green, brown or even stripes.

Katmai National Park contains salmon streams.

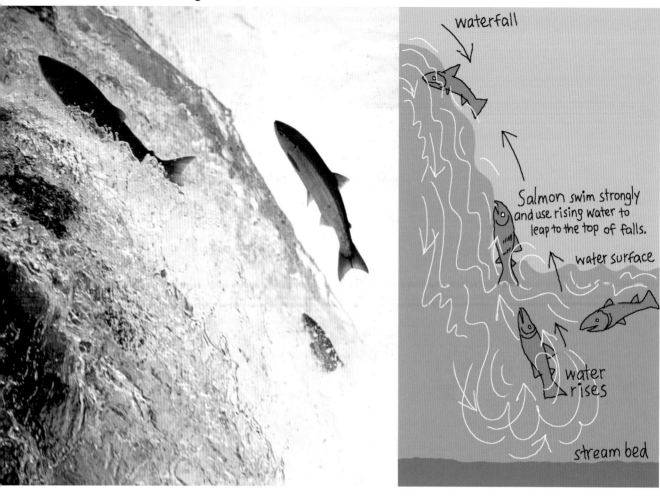

waterfall

Salmon swim strongly and use rising water to leap to the top of falls.

water surface

water rises

stream bed

At the waterfall

Soon the salmon reach the most difficult and dangerous part of their journey. They arrive at a waterfall. All around the base of the falls, salmon are leaping out of the water. Some leap many times higher than their own body length, but this is not enough for them to reach the top of these falls. They swim about the bottom of the falls, searching for the places where the most water is falling.

The water that plunges over the falls goes deeply into the stream bed then rises towards the surface. The salmon use this force by diving deeply and swimming strongly upward with the rising water, getting an added push from the energy of the falls.

In this way, they can sometimes overcome the force of the falling water and reach the top of the falls.

Some fish do this easily, while others make many attempts before they succeed. But for some, the power of the water is too great and they never reach the spawning grounds, and they die without ever spawning.

Danger awaits

As well as these difficulties, there are also many dangers. Predators, such as bears, gather around the waterfall and other places where the salmon are held up by difficult river or stream conditions.

 Did you know?

In the big rivers, some salmon travel as many as 1,600 kilometres upstream before they reach their destination. These fish swim about 30 to 50 kilometres each day.

Pacific salmon timeline

 Early summer
Salmon swim from Pacific Ocean to streams in Alaska

Predators at the falls

Smaller, younger bears compete for the remains of the fish.

A mother bear teaches her two young cubs how to fish.

Salmon leap out of the water, trying to reach the top of the waterfall.

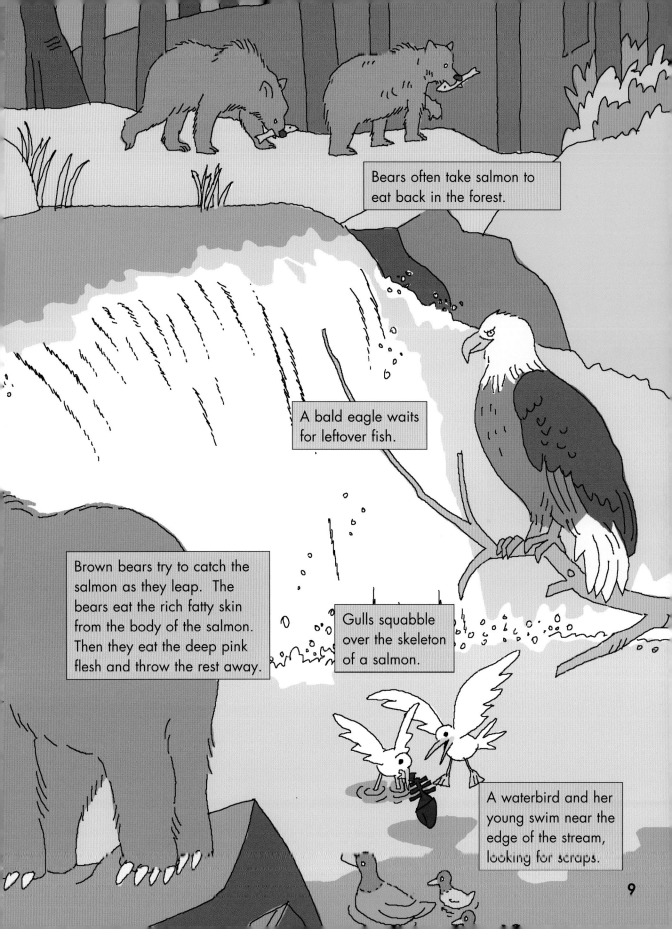

Bears often take salmon to eat back in the forest.

A bald eagle waits for leftover fish.

Brown bears try to catch the salmon as they leap. The bears eat the rich fatty skin from the body of the salmon. Then they eat the deep pink flesh and throw the rest away.

Gulls squabble over the skeleton of a salmon.

A waterbird and her young swim near the edge of the stream, looking for scraps.

At the spawning grounds

Even though many salmon cannot reach the top of the falls or are caught by the bears, enough of the fish manage to continue upstream to the quiet waters of their spawning grounds.

Digging the nest

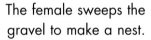

The female sweeps the gravel to make a nest.

When salmon arrive at their spawning grounds in the autumn, the females begin looking for a place to build a nest. The female faces upstream and turns on her side, sweeping the stream bed with powerful movements of her tail. This moves gravel and loosens dirt and other lighter materials that the current carries downstream.

A nest may be up to 60 centimetres long and 45 centimetres deep, depending on the salmon species. Male partners guard the nest and try to keep intruders away. During this time, the eggs ripen inside the body of the female and she becomes larger and fatter than the male.

Salmon facts: Types and features of Pacific salmon

	Species	Weight (kg)	Lifetime (years)	Eggs	Incubation (weeks)
	Pink (humpback)	2	2	1,500	7–10
	Sockeye (red)	3	4–5	4,000	6–9
	Chum (dog)	4	3–5	2,500	8
	Coho (silver)	6	3	2,500	6–7
	Chinook (king)	25	5–7	8,500	12

Spawning

The nest is ready some weeks after the salmon reach the spawning grounds. Now the female swims towards the nest, with the male close behind. She lays several thousand eggs in the hole, which the male **fertilises**.

The female then moves a little further upstream and begins digging a new nest. As she digs, the stream carries some of the dirt and gravel to the first nest and covers the eggs. Females continue to dig nests until all their eggs are laid. Each female lays between 1,500 and 10,000 eggs, depending on the species (see chart on page 10).

A lifetime ends

After the eggs are laid, males and females begin to drift downstream. They have not eaten since they left the ocean and the food supply stored in their bodies is gone. Their lives are almost over as their bodies waste away. Their skins are now a sickly white colour, their scales drop off, and their fins fall apart. The purpose of their journey is achieved, as they have left behind millions of new salmon waiting to be born. Salmon on the Pacific coast never survive to spawn a second time.

▲ Salmon eggs (enlarged)

▲ Dead salmon on a riverbank

Pacific salmon timeline

Early summer
Salmon swim from Pacific Ocean to streams in Alaska

Autumn
Adult salmon nest and spawn

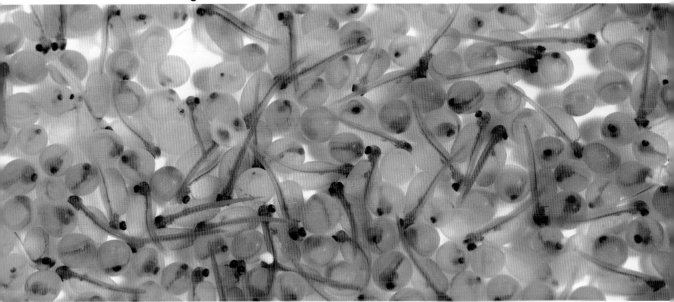

Salmon eggs beginning to hatch

A new lifetime begins

The eggs in the stream bed develop slowly through the winter.
The first signs of life begin after about a month, when the eyes
start to appear. They look like little black specks in the eggs.
Next, the shape of a fish appears and a small red dot beats under
the throat – this is the heart. An orange yolk sac attached under
the growing **embryo** provides all its nourishment.

Hatching

Finally, in late winter, the embryo has grown too big for the egg.
The tail breaks through and a young fish hatches from the egg.
These tiny creatures are called alevins. They have huge eyes and
continue to feed from the yolk sac until they use up all the food in
the sac. Then, when they are bigger and stronger, they leave the
gravel nest that has protected them from predators. A good flow
of pure water is also needed for the alevins to develop successfully.

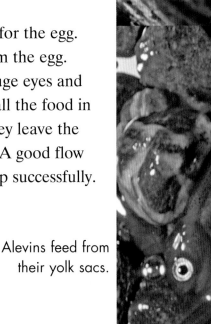

Alevins feed from
their yolk sacs.

Newly emerged fry

Alevins emerge from the gravel as they lose their sacs in the spring. The fish are now called fry. They are about two centimetres long. The coming of spring in the salmon stream brings new food, such as insects and tiny plants and animals called plankton. Without parents to look after them, the young fry must find their own food and avoid predators.

Fry have vertical bars called parr marks on their sides, which help them remain **camouflaged** from predators. The fry spend up to a year in the stream and grow up to 13 centimetres in length. Many are eaten by predators.

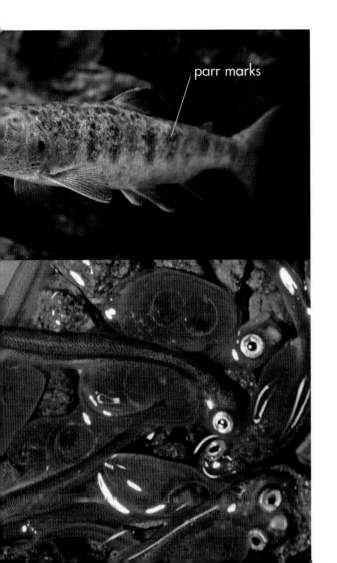

parr marks

Pacific salmon timeline

Early summer
Salmon swim from Pacific Ocean to streams in Alaska

Autumn
Adult salmon nest and spawn

Winter
Eggs develop

Spring
Alevins emerge from gravel

Sockeye salmon

Moving downstream

As they **migrate** downstream in spring towards the salt water, the young salmon begin to make the changes they will need for life in the ocean. They spend some time in places where the fresh water of a stream or river meets salt water.

These young salmon are called smoults. Their bodies change from a brown colour with dark stripes to a silvery colour that will help camouflage them in the ocean. Their scales become larger, and their tails grow longer and more forked. They become much stronger and can swim very well. But this is a very dangerous time for smoults, as many are eaten by predators such as birds and seals.

Salmon life cycle

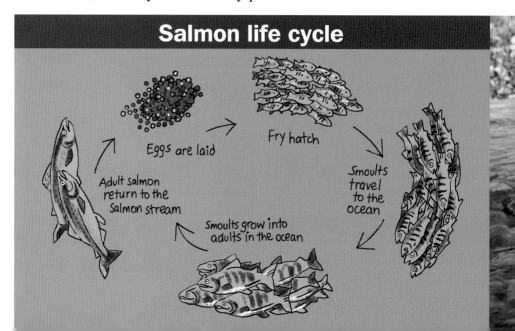

Eggs are laid

Fry hatch

Smoults travel to the ocean

Adult salmon return to the salmon stream

Smoults grow into adults in the ocean

Living in the ocean

Pacific salmon **mature** in the open ocean. Some species travel up to 3,000 kilometres from the coast, but others stay much closer to land. By the time they reach the age of two years, most salmon have completely **adapted** to living in the ocean. They have sharp teeth, hard protective scales and very strong jaws. They eat small fish such as herring and anchovies, as well as squid and shrimp.

After about four years at sea, salmon are fully grown. Soon the urge to find the stream of their birth and start the next **generation** overcomes them, and they begin their last great journey.

Chinook salmon

Ocean predators

During the ocean stage of their life cycles, adult salmon face danger from larger fish such as swordfish and tuna, as well as seals, sea lions, dolphins and killer whales, which are their major predators.

Pacific salmon timeline

 Early summer
Salmon swim from Pacific Ocean to streams in Alaska

 Autumn
Adult salmon nest and spawn

 Winter
Eggs develop

 Spring
Alevins emerge. Smolts swim downstream. Young adult salmon swim to ocean.

 1–4 years later
Salmon swim from Pacific Ocean to streams in Alaska

Chapter 2

A grizzly predator

The bears that fish for salmon at the waterfall belong to a **species** called brown bears. These brown bears are known as grizzly bears. This name comes from the appearance of their long coats, which are tipped with lighter coloured hairs that give them a "grizzled" look.

Size

Along with polar bears, brown bears are the largest land predators on Earth. Females are much smaller and reach about half to three-quarters the size of males. The weight of a brown bear varies a great deal during the year. They are lightest in the spring and early summer, and heaviest at the end of autumn.

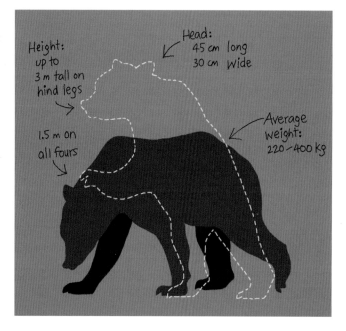

Height: up to 3 m tall on hind legs

1.5 m on all fours

Head: 45 cm long 30 cm wide

Average weight: 220–400 kg

Head

Brown bears have huge muscles in their head to work their powerful jaws. They have small ears to reduce the loss of their body heat. Their sharp sense of hearing allows them to find animals that live under the ground. Their large mouths contain teeth that are used both for tearing meat and grinding plants. Brown bears have good eyesight and an excellent sense of smell.

Feet and legs

Brown bears have large, flat feet that stop them from sinking far into the snow. The soles of their feet are padded and covered with thick, tough leather. The claws on the front feet are up to 15 centimetres long and are curved to help them dig. They keep their claws sharp by scratching them into tree bark. They use their claws to pick berries, dig for small animals and catch fish. Brown bears have massive leg bones and shoulders, with a shoulder hump of muscle to power their front legs. Brown bears can move very quickly for their size and can travel long distances without a rest.

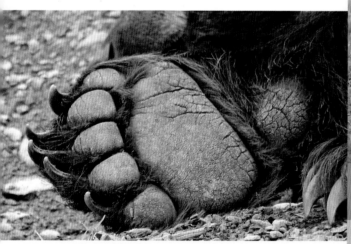

Bear facts

Class: Mammal
Family: Bear
Scientific name: Ursus arctos
Common name: Brown bear
Average weight: 200–400 kilograms
Number of cubs: 2–3 cubs born every 3–5 years
Life expectancy: Up to 22–26 years

17

Feeding

Brown bears are omnivores, which means they eat both animals and plants. They are always hungry, and for much of the year they spend most of their day munching on grass, flowers and berries. About 80 per cent of their diet is plants. In seven months they have to eat enough food to last them for the whole year, including the time when they are **hibernating** in their den for up to five months.

Spring and summer

When they emerge from their dens in spring after the long winter, brown bears are very hungry. With their strong sense of smell, they find bulbs underground, even under thick snow. They dig up roots, tubers, grasses, buds and leaves. They turn over rocks and boulders, eating centipedes and beetles. They also prey on young animals such as moose, elk, deer, caribou and ground squirrels.

In May, mothers and cubs eat a plant called horsetail, which grows near pools, and eat muskrats that get too close. They churn up and turn over green meadows as they dig for small rodents called voles. Brown bears living near the coast move towards the salmon streams in June to gorge themselves on the fish that **migrate**.

By August there are fewer salmon available, and the bears' diet shifts towards fruits and fresh pine nuts from cones that have been buried in holes by squirrels. They may even eat the squirrels. Brown bears eat many kinds of berries. They may spend time high on the mountains or in the river valleys.

Autumn

By September the **salmon runs** have finished, and the bears must now eat plants. When October arrives, food is hard to find. Green plants are dead; marmots and ground squirrels are already hibernating; pocket gophers have gone deep into winter tunnels. Brown bears begin to prepare and dig their winter dens. Pregnant females are the first to go into dens.

Cranberries

Blueberries

Huckleberries

Preparing to hibernate

Brown bears normally dig their own dens, although they sometimes use a cave or a hollow tree. They dig into a remote slope, usually beneath a large tree with plenty of rock or soil overhead to form a thick roof. The bear burrows straight into the slope, throwing out large amounts of rock and soil.

The tunnel is barely big enough for the bear to squeeze through. At the end of this tunnel, the bear then digs out a larger space where it will spend the winter. There is just enough room to curl up tightly and sometimes change position.

Digging the den usually takes between three and seven days. Some bears take a long time searching for bedding and preparing the den. Spruce and fir branches are used for bedding, along with moss and grass. The den opening is then clogged and covered by a heavy blanket of snow that hides it and keeps the cold out.

Hibernation

Brown bears fall into a light sleep during hibernation but they can be awakened during this time. Some hibernating animals fall into a deep sleep and cannot be awakened until spring. Like other bears that hibernate, brown bears can store great amounts of food in their body for use during hibernation. During these months, their body temperature, heart rate, breathing and energy use fall as their bodies slow down.

Staying alive

Throughout the winter, these bears do not eat, drink, **defecate** or **urinate**. They live off their fat reserves and their bodies re-use waste products. Before going to their dens, they eat up to 83,000 kilojoules per day to fatten themselves up. During hibernation a bear will use about 16,000 kilojoules per day.

The brown bear's year

Spring

Bears emerge from their dens. They are very hungry and plenty of food is available.

leaves

buds

sedges and grasses

muskrats

voles

March

April

May

Summer

Food is still plentiful.

berries

marmots

salmon

squirrels

pine nuts

June

July

August

Autumn

Food is becoming scarce; bears eat whatever plants they can find. Bears prepare their dens.

plants

September

October

November

Winter

Bears spend the winter in their dens. Pregnant females give birth to young.

December

January

February

A new life begins

Brown bears mate during the months of May through July. The young do not begin to grow inside the mother until hibernation starts. They grow inside their mother for six to ten weeks.

The cubs are born in January or February while the mother is still hibernating. The cubs are so tiny that they hardly look like bears. They are blind, nearly hairless, toothless, weigh less than 450 grams and are almost helpless. Sometimes only one cub is born, but there may be as many as four. The tiny cubs feed on their mother's milk and grow very quickly.

Mothers emerge from the den with their cubs in about mid-April. By now the cubs weigh about two kilograms. Young brown bears feed on their mother's milk for 18 months to two and a half years.

Growing up

Brown bear cubs are very playful. As young cubs they like to stay close to their mothers, although they will chase each other or other animals, such as caribou. They soon grow fat in summer and develop a sleek coat.

The mother bears may feed for 18 to 20 hours a day. They eat an enormous amount of food to produce milk and the cubs gain weight very quickly. In August the cubs weigh about 27 kilograms each and by October they weigh about 45 kilograms. As the cold weather sets in, the mother digs a new den for all the family and the bear cubs spend the second winter of their lives with her in the den.

When spring comes again, the mothers play with the cubs, discipline them and teach them. During this second spring of their lives, if the mother is ready to mate, she forces her cubs to leave her and look after themselves. Even with their mother's protection and knowledge of where to find food, up to 40 per cent of cubs die during their first year of life.

 Did you know?

A 225-kilogram brown bear has cubs that weigh around half a kilogram each. This is about 1/400th as much as their mother. A newborn human weighs about 1/20th as much as its mother.

Chapter 3 Needing each other

The lifetime of the Pacific salmon and the lifetime of the brown bear come together in a very dramatic way when the salmon **migrate**. At first it seems like a terrible end for the salmon, to battle its way to the top of the waterfall close to its breeding grounds only to be taken by a huge bear. It's easy to see how the bears benefit from the salmon, but there are also benefits to the salmon and to the whole environment through which the salmon stream flows.

How salmon help brown bears and other animals

During summer, brown bears that live near salmon streams mostly eat salmon. Studies done by scientists show that each bear eats about 720 salmon during the migration season. Because each bear eats about half of each salmon, that leaves more than 6,000 kilograms of fish to be eaten by other animals. Bears prefer particular parts of the salmon, such as the brains, skin, flesh and eggs. The leftover salmon is eaten by younger bears and other wildlife such as bald eagles, gulls, minks and river otters.

During summer, the migrating salmon are the major food source for a large population of bears and many smaller animals. Apart from mothers with cubs, brown bears are normally **solitary** animals. However, between 50 and 60 can live together in the small environment around the salmon stream during the salmon migration.

25

Brown bears eat only about half of the salmon they capture. Some of the carcass is eaten by other animals or is left on the forest floor, where it decomposes. As the salmon rots, nitrogen that has built up in the body of these fish is released and is absorbed into the soil. This nitrogen is then taken up by the roots of trees and other plants.

How salmon and bears help the environment

Bears also move the salmon they catch from the streams into the forest. Mothers with cubs and younger bears usually take their catch from the stream to a place in the nearby spruce forest to avoid threats and thefts from larger bears.

Scientists have found that each bear hauls about 1,500 kilograms of fish into the forest. They think that 55 tonnes of salmon per year are moved from the streams of British Columbia, in Canada, into the forest **ecosystem**. The bodies of the salmon contain an important plant food called **nitrogen**. About half the nitrogen in trees within 90 metres of the salmon stream came from the ocean. So the spruce trees and other plants in this ecosystem are getting important **nutrients** because of the actions of the salmon and the bears.

How bears help salmon

Depending on the **species**, each female salmon may lay about 5,000 eggs in her lifetime. If all these eggs hatched and survived to **reproduce**, the rivers and oceans would quickly be overrun with salmon and most would die from starvation. But that does not happen.

Not all of the eggs grow. Some of the eggs are eaten by predators. Some of the alevins die or are eaten by predators. Many of the fry are also eaten by predators. Lots of the smolt do not make the change from a freshwater to a saltwater life. Not all of the salmon survive the years in the ocean to make the long journey upstream. And still others do not survive the journey upstream. In the end, as few as two salmon out of the 5,000 eggs return to their birth stream to spawn.

Brown bears have an important role to play in this amazing lifetime. They help to make sure that only the strongest, fittest salmon are able to make it to the **spawning grounds** to begin the next **generation**.

Did you know?

One type of nitrogen is found only in the oceans and this type of nitrogen has been found up to 450 metres from the salmon streams.

Chapter 4

Tourists and salmon streams

Salmon streams are prized places for tourists to visit because they are usually in very beautiful, wild places. People enjoy fishing in these streams, and many people go there hoping to see bears in numbers that are normally not seen in the wild. Some **environmentalists**, however, believe that tourists damage the environment and that the bears should be left alone. Other people believe that brown bears are too dangerous to be around humans.

However, tourists can visit salmon streams safely and without damaging the environment.

Find out more

Find out when the bears can be seen live on webcam at Brooks Falls. View and describe their activities.

Brooks Camp

A successful example of how to manage tourists in these areas can be found at Brooks Camp in Katmai National Park in Alaska. The people in charge of this camp make sure tourists understand how to stay safe and how to protect the environment.

KATMAI NATIONAL PARK

RULES

✗ Do not take food outside the dining room or camping ground.

✗ Do not carry food on walking trips close to the river and falls area.

✗ Do not clean fish that are caught. Fish must be placed in sealed plastic bags and frozen until visitors leave.

HOW TO BEHAVE AROUND BEARS

✔ Keep a safe distance between people and bears.

✔ When walking through the forest, make a lot of noise to avoid surprising bears.

Visitors arrive by seaplane or boat and must report to the Park Service Visitors Centre, where rangers explain and show tourists a video on how to behave when bears are around. Rangers also explain the rules of the national park.

The camping ground has an electric fence around it so bears cannot get in. Bears quickly learn to associate human and rubbish smells with food, and this creates danger for both. If they become a problem around rubbish, the bears may be taken away from the national park.

Viewing areas

In the main places where bears and people come closer together, special areas have been built to make sure people are safe and the bears are not disturbed. There is a large viewing platform at the falls that keeps people safe from the bears and gives them an excellent view of the bears and the salmon.

The viewing platform at Brooks River

There is also a bridge across the Brooks River with a viewing platform and safety area. Rangers are on duty during daylight hours and the bridge is closed whenever bears come close to it. There are limits on the number of tourists who can come to the area. The needs of the bears come before the needs of the tourists.

The management of the area has been successful in preventing injuries to both bears and people. There have been a few problems and some bears have been removed from the area. Brooks Camp shows that tourists and bears can mix successfully when the things that cause problems are controlled.

Glossary

adapted   changed to suit the environment

camouflaged   hidden among its surroundings

current   the flowing movement of a section of water

defecate   expel faeces from the body

ecosystem   a whole community of living things that depend on each other for survival

embryo   an animal that is just starting to develop

environmentalist   a person who works to protect the natural environment

fertilises   adds sperm to make eggs grow

generation   a group of people or animals born around the same time

hibernating   sleeping through winter; some animals fall into a heavy sleep but others doze or sleep lightly

incubation   the time that eggs take to hatch

mature   become fully grown

migrate   move from one area to another

nitrogen   a chemical element found in all living things; nitrogen gas makes up 80 per cent of the earth's atmosphere

nutrients   ingredients in food that keep living things alive

rapids   part of a river where the water moves quickly and can be rough

reproduce   produce young of its kind

salmon runs   movements of salmon from the ocean through the mountain streams

solitary   alone

spawning grounds   areas where fish go to lay eggs

species   a group of very closely related animals that can reproduce with each other

urinate   expel urine from the body

Index